Lessons of an Effective Nonprofit Executive: Chasing Community Change

Perry Gunn

Dedication

I dedicate this book to my beloved family—my wife of 40 years, Sharon, and my children, Rashonda, Sherry, Ryan, and Jasmine, who have sustained me throughout my career with their unwavering support. Their encouragement kept me focused on my mission, my goals, and the work I felt called to do.

I am deeply grateful to my mentors and the leaders who believed in me, including Victor M., Paul B., James H., Bill K., Dr. Kate G., John L., and Steve D. I also extend heartfelt thanks to the talented teams I had the privilege of leading and working with as we served some of Chicago's most underserved communities, including Cabrini Green, Stateway Gardens, Altgeld Gardens, and Englewood.

A special tribute goes to my late parents, Minnie and Peter, as well as my siblings Barbara, Brenda, Debbie, Diane, Lisa, Tanzella, Larry, and Glennard, who preceded me in death, and the Whitfield family, who shaped my values and character from the very beginning. They instilled in me the passion and commitment to serve my community—guiding principles that have carried me through every chapter of this journey.

It has been a remarkable ride, one that captured my heart from the very start and never let go.

If you're reading this e-book, you're standing at the threshold of one of the most demanding and consequential roles in our society. Perhaps you're preparing to step into nonprofit leadership for the first time. Maybe you already serve as a CEO and are searching for clarity, strength, or renewal. Or perhaps someone who sees your potential has told you, "You'd be great at this."

My name is Perry Gunn, and I am a veteran. I spent forty years in the trenches of nonprofit leadership. Let me be direct: guiding a nonprofit organization is not a casual stroll. It is complex, high-stakes, deeply human work that will stretch you in ways you never expected.

Leading a nonprofit is a bit like steering a ship through ever-changing waters—rewarding, mission-driven, and undeniably complex. Effective leadership demands a rare blend of strategy, empathy, and operational discipline. This e-book is your roadmap, built from decades of lived experience, offering the essential practices you need to help lead your organization from a solid entity to a sustainable institution that delivers real, lasting impact in your community.

And because stories are often the best teachers, I'll share plenty of them—moments that shaped me, challenged me, and taught me what it truly means to lead. Some will inspire you. Some may make you laugh. All of them will offer practical wisdom from someone who has spent a lifetime doing this work.

Settle in. There's a lot to learn and even more to gain. I hope you enjoy the journey.

Table of Contents

Chapter 1: The Beginning and Summary of the Journey

My passion for working with young people began early. At just 12 years old, I found myself coaching baseball alongside my peers. Hearing a young person call me "Coach" for the first time was unforgettable—it amazed me that I could already be someone who offered guidance and support.

By the time I turned 16, I knew I wanted to become a youth practitioner. I asked my youth leader, Victor, how I could turn that passion into a real career. Victor was an amazing youth leader who pointed me toward a college dedicated to preparing future YMCA professionals and social workers.

Once I arrived there, everything clicked. I gained skills that shaped not only my professional path but also my sense of purpose. I felt fully prepared to lead and empower youth anywhere in the world. I was confident, energized, and eager to begin the work I knew I wanted to do.

In 1978, I turned "pro". I accepted a job as a Professional Youth Worker with the Boys and Girls Clubs of Detroit. My sister was hesitant about my accepting this appointment since she told me that I needed to get a real job. My response was, “I do have a real job. In fact, I will have the opportunity to make a difference by helping young people who are hanging out on the streets become individuals who hold on to the positive values they will learn at the club."

At the Boys and Girls Clubs of Detroit, I honed my programming skills, learning to develop programs of the highest standards to meet participants' needs. I mastered program planning, program delivery, record keeping, and other leadership skills.

I spent several years at the Boys and Girls Clubs of Detroit before relocating back to Chicago, where I accepted a role as the Youth Program Director with the YMCA of Chicago. In this position, I continued developing my program development skills while also beginning to explore executive roles. I applied to become an executive at a central YMCA Center and was appointed the Executive Director of the Youth and Community Development Center. I was 30 years old and one of the youngest executives in the system.

Stepping into my first leadership role was far more challenging than I expected. Some of the older staff questioned my authority, and many struggled to buy in because I wasn't yet communicating roles and responsibilities clearly. For the first three months, I found myself frustrated by disrespect, insubordination, and a poor work ethic. I knew something had to change, so I reached out to my Executive Director, Jim, for guidance.

Jim gave me some of the best leadership advice I've ever received. He told me, "Stop carrying the work in my agenda and instead make it our work." He encouraged me to seek the team's input, build shared goals, and let them lead alongside me. Then he said something I still remember vividly: "I don't mean to be this frank, but you have the ink pen, not them. If you need to write someone up for being disrespectful or insubordinate, your pen works. They'll get the message."

His words sparked a new confidence in me. I began engaging the team with clarity, purpose, and a renewed sense of authority. I challenged them respectfully but firmly, and they responded. Slowly, the culture shifted. The team became more accountable, more collaborative, and more invested in our shared success.

It was during this period of growth that I also discovered my talent for fundraising. I became highly effective at securing major gifts, winning grants, and leading large-scale special events. I was fortunate to be mentored by our Vice President, who I still believe is one of the best fundraisers in the world. That mentorship, combined with the leadership lessons I learned early on, shaped me into the professional I am today.

At this YMCA, I was part of a team that raised millions of dollars annually, and our special event (the Bonanza Auction) generated $2,500,000 in one night. It was also here that I learned that the YMCA is bigger than the four walls that contain it. I began to understand collaboration, outreach, and partnerships. I created a community-wide tutoring program that operated in churches, schools, youth centers, and within public housing projects. Overall, this program was very successful because it met a critical community need at the time.

Furthermore, I created the Refrigeration Repair Program in response to a community leader's request to repair refrigerators and assist many residents struggling with diabetes promptly. I trained 30 residents in refrigeration repair by networking with my Board members from Sears Roebuck and Washburne Trade School, who created a customized training program for the residents. After training several residents, I secured a multi-year contract with the Chicago Housing Authority, enabling all trainees to secure full-time employment.

I left this position after three years because the community asked me to lead a Chicago Youth Center in the heart of Cabrini Green, a neighborhood considered one of the most dangerous in the country. I was hesitant to take the position because of all the success I was having at the YMCA, but in the end, I accepted it and looked forward to the challenge.

Gangs controlled this youth center, which sat inside one gang's territory, only 400 yards from a rival group. On the first day that I reopened the center, I remember one gang leader pointing out to others that I had left one of the premier YMCAs to work at this youth center. Later, that same person told me that several youth had guns when they came to programming on the first day, and that I needed a system to ensure everyone's safety. The next day, I checked everyone in, making sure no one had any guns, and all males removed their hats. That was the beginning of us taking control of the facility and setting overall expectations for the future. When I took over, there was graffiti all around the building, but after we cleaned it all up. The graffiti never returned because of the trust my team established with the community. I went on to raise significant funding and build a strong Board of Directors.

I moved forward with my journey, having worked in several small community-based entities and later returning to the YMCA as Vice President of Operations, where I oversaw the Chicago YMCA sites and several suburban locations. Once again, I was a successful fundraiser even though that was not my primary role. I became highly effective in building community collaborations and partnerships.

I concluded my professional career at Teamwork Englewood, one of the most rewarding roles I've ever held. But the beginning was anything but smooth. The organization lacked trust within the broader community, and several neighborhood groups believed we were monopolizing resources. To make matters more complicated, our service area included six Aldermen, each with their own priorities and political dynamics. I didn't move quickly enough to build relationships with these public officials, and as a result, the narrative of mistrust continued to grow.

Although I was the new leader, many community groups didn't notice a difference right away. That changed once I deliberately made the effort to get out into the neighborhood, meet people where they were, and set a new tone for how we would operate. I clearly communicated the organization's intention to partner with residents and collaborate with local stakeholders to make Englewood a better place to live, work, and do business. As my team and I made our rounds across the community, perceptions shifted quickly.

I loved being on the ground, building genuine partnerships, and working on real issues that mattered to residents. During my tenure, I led a successful community-wide planning process that engaged thousands of residents in shaping their neighborhood's future. That plan—still active today—continues to drive progress in public safety, housing, reentry, health, economic development, youth development, and education.

Under my leadership, we tripled the organization's budget, strengthened our partnership with a highly engaged Board, and implemented a thoughtful succession plan to ensure long-term sustainability. Because of that planning, the organization has since tripled its budget again and continues to thrive and grow.

When I officially retired, I started the Nonprofit Membership Club, an organization that allows me to share my wisdom and knowledge about this work with grassroots and other nonprofit organizations.

The following chapters will provide lessons and strategies for becoming effective in a nonprofit leadership role.

Key Life Lessons: The Wisdom of Mentors; The Value of Developing Marketable Skills; The Courage to Face Adversaries; Innovation Sparks Commitment; Catalyzing a Team is Always a Winning Strategy

Chapter 2: What's Your Mission, Vision, and Values?

As a nonprofit leader, your work will address a critical societal issue. In approaching this effort, you must establish a culture, build trust, and mobilize people to make a difference in the community. Setting the organizational foundation starts with a clear mission statement. A good mission statement tells everyone why your organization exists. I recommend limiting mission statements to 35 words or fewer. It should be concise and clearly written.

Overall, a compelling **mission** statement offers several benefits, including the following:

- Helping to guide strategic priorities
- Ensuring alignment across programs
- Attracting staff, volunteers, and donors

Your **vision** statement offers an aspirational look at where you want your organization to be down the road, in other words, where you hope the agency will land when it grows up. A powerful vision statement is:

- **Future-focused** — describes the world you want to help build
- **Inspiring** — energizes staff, donors, and the community

- **Clear and concise** — easy to remember and repeat
- **Ambitious but achievable** — bold, yet grounded in your mission
- **Impact-oriented** — centered on the change you want to see

Nonprofit ***values*** are the guiding principles that shape how an organization serves its community, makes decisions, and treats its stakeholders. They're the heartbeat of mission-driven work. When a nonprofit lives its values well, you can feel it in its culture, programs, and relationships.

Key Life Lessons: A mission is a vital organizing principle for leaders; Mission, vision, and values are the pillars of leadership

Chapter 3: Getting the right Board on the Bus

Let's be honest: nonprofit boards are like an extended family. You love them. You appreciate them. But sometimes you need to take a walk around the block before responding to their emails.

A great board is a gift. A dysfunctional board is cardio.

But here's the good news: you can shape your Board into a powerhouse—one that governs well, supports you, and doesn't try to run the day-to-day operations as if they're auditioning for "Nonprofit Survivor."

It requires:

- **Clear expectations**
- **Strong relationships**
- **Regular communication**
- **And the courage to say, "That's a great idea for staff, not the board."**

I always start by identifying the right mix of individuals to serve on my Board. My first step is to organize a board recruitment event to bring in potential members who fit the profile and possess the specific skills evident in successful boards. For example, all my effective boards included three types of individuals:

Grinders, the worker bees. These individuals are consistent in handling a variety of tasks within the organization, and you can count on them as reliable resources to get the organization's work done.

Minders are members who mind the affairs of the organization. These board members ensure the agency remains in good standing. They ensure the organization spends funds correctly, stays true to its mission, operates ethically and transparently, and complies with all laws.

Finders are members who focus on finding resources and funding to carry out the organization's mission effectively. These individuals have access to influential relationships, leverage their professional connections, make introductions to the funding community, and advocate with various public and private entities on behalf of the agency.

When you have a good balance of Grinders, Minders, and Finders, you have the key ingredients to establish and maintain a solid board for many years.

Key Life Lessons: Mobilize A Leadership Support System Based On Collective Goals And Individual Talents

Chapter 4: Fundraising with a Plan & Purpose

Fundraising is one of the most defining and most draining responsibilities for a nonprofit executive. It's not just about asking for money; it's about navigating a complex ecosystem of donors, staff, board members, community expectations, and limited resources. When you peel back the layers, the challenges are both strategic and deeply human.

Here's a clear, structured look at the biggest hurdles nonprofit leaders face, along with the underlying dynamics that make them so persistent.

1. Balancing mission and money. You're constantly walking a tightrope between staying true to your mission and securing funding to pursue it.

2. Your nonprofit faces stiff competition in a crowded field of charities competing for attention.

3. Funders face a constant flood of requests as the economy rises and falls.

4. You don't have a team or the capacity to handle fundraising tasks, such as individual campaigns, special events, cultivation, data collection and management, and relationship building.

5. Your Board is supposed to be a partner in the fundraising endeavor, but many members are uncomfortable asking for money.
6. The organization still holds you accountable for fundraising outcomes, even though it should be a shared burden.

Fortunately, there are steps you can take to strengthen your ability to become successful in fundraising as the CEO/Executive Director of a Nonprofit. Here are some of the steps I routinely carried out throughout my career.

1. Start by developing a comprehensive fundraising plan that defines a realistic fundraising goal, specifies funding strategies for individuals, foundations, special events, and government, outlines a work plan that identifies leadership team responsibilities, and establishes Key Performance Indicators to measure the success of your plan.

A strong fundraising plan is one of the most powerful tools a nonprofit can have. It's not just a document—it's the roadmap that keeps your mission funded, your team aligned, and your organization resilient when the environment shifts. When a nonprofit operates without one, it's essentially relying on hope instead of strategy.

2. Commit to spending at least 60% of your time on fundraising activities such as donor cultivation, solicitation, and making the "ask," stewardship, Board engagement, and Networking. You must focus on getting out into the community rather than the day-to-day operations. **Important Lesson:** Throughout my career, I figured out how to get into the room with individual donors, foundations, and

government supporters. To do this, I consistently looked for events that foundations hosted or public officials held, and I sought out invitations to private donor homes from my network of high-profile donors and Board members who kept company with the wealthy.

Additionally, I ensured all donors remained informed about the organization's program successes by sending annual reports, impact reports, and personal notes. When you can provide effective stewardship, it helps to build trust and credibility with your funders.

3. Always keep a case for support at your fingertips. You must tell compelling stories and be ready to give your elevator pitch on the spot. Your elevator pitch should include a **hook** statement to grab the attention of the person you are speaking to about your organization. It can be a rhetorical question or specific data and facts about the issue your agency addresses. It should include a **body** statement that explains how your organization is addressing the problem, and a quick synopsis of your agency's credentials. Finally, your elevator pitch should conclude with a **wrap-up** statement that offers the person a way to get involved with the organization. For example, a statement like "It has been a pleasure to meet you today." "Would you like to learn more about how you can become involved with our organization?"

4. You must make a concerted effort to diversify your revenue streams. If you are sitting back and relying solely on grants or special events, you will have long days and struggle to sustain your work. A balance of income coming into your organization can protect the mission for many years.

Key Life Lessons: Have a Plan and Work the Plan; Be in the Room or Create the Room; Be One with a Compelling Message: Mission Generates Money

Chapter 5: Leading a Team that Matters

In nonprofit work, a mission becomes real only when a committed team brings it to life day after day. Impact doesn't happen by accident—it happens when a leader can mobilize people by inspiring them, building authentic relationships, trusting them to own their roles, and cultivating a culture where collaboration and proactive change feel possible.

Strong nonprofit leadership isn't about authority; it's about creating the conditions where people *want* to contribute their best.

Key Lessons in Leading a Mission-Driven Team

- **Communicate clearly and consistently** so everyone understands priorities, expectations, and goals.
- **Be transparent in decision-making**—let your team in on the "why," not just the "what."
- **Recognize wins and meaningful contributions**, both big and small.
- **Develop leaders from within** by delegating opportunities that stretch skills and build confidence.
- **Provide real pathways for professional growth**, not just in title but in experience and learning.

A Story About Team Building

When I created the Learning Enrichment Tutoring (LET) program at Cabrini-Green Housing Development, it began as a Saturday initiative staffed entirely by volunteers. What made it extraordinary was that my team, without being asked or assigned, chose to run the program for years without compensation. They believed so deeply in the program's purpose that they planned, staffed, and sustained it themselves.

For at least three years, a dedicated group of staff and volunteers operated the LET program simply because they believed in the mission.

Their commitment revealed something powerful: they invested themselves in the work, the youth, and the vision of what was possible. That team became one of the strongest youth development groups in Chicago, and many of its members have since gone on to become nonprofit directors across the city.

Key Life Lesson: Team Synergy Is the Ideal Leadership Goal

Chapter 6: Managing the Money is the Real Deal

It's not uncommon for a nonprofit executive to tense up when they hear terms like *audits, profit and loss statements, cash reserves, cash flow, restricted funding*, or *overhead.* You might even think to yourself, "I'm not the accountant—why do I need to know this?" As the CEO or Executive Director, you don't need to *be* the accountant, but it is essential that you fully understand the numbers. Financial literacy allows you to make informed decisions, provide effective oversight, and ensure the long-term health of the organization. It also helps you develop a strong organizational budget and a realistic program plan.

Key lessons for effective financial management include:

- **Ensure your Board approves an annual budget** that includes reliable revenue sources and thoughtful cash-flow forecasting.
- **Prepare an Organizational Budget Summary** that provides the Board and key stakeholders with a clear, written narrative explaining what the numbers mean. A narrative helps answer questions and paints a clearer picture of your intentions.

- **Commit to balancing your operating budget each year.** Ongoing deficits can lead to grant denials and other serious challenges.

- **Meet regularly with your finance team** to understand the organization's financial position and to plan corrective actions when needed.
- **Have an external party review the books if you manage them yourself,** to ensure transparency and integrity.
- **Develop financial policies** that support proper compliance with accounting standards and all applicable laws.

A Story About the Finances

In my second week as Executive Director of a community organization, the business manager walked into my office and said, "Payroll needs to be processed tomorrow." I told her to go ahead—only to hear, "I can't. We don't have enough funds in the account to cover payroll."

I was stunned. I had thoroughly reviewed the organization's books before accepting the role. But the reality is that books can look a certain way, even when the truth is far less stable. And now, just two weeks into my leadership, I was facing a crisis that could send the entire staff into panic.

During my interview process, a Board member—who happened to work at the bank across the street—mentioned that the bank was an annual supporter, typically giving around $25,000 each September.

Well, it was July, and I needed a solution immediately. So, I walked across the street, explained the situation, and politely asked whether the bank could provide their annual gift early so we could meet payroll.

He said he would check. Later that afternoon, he confirmed that the bank could indeed release the $25,000 right away.

I saved payroll, but the experience taught me a lesson I've carried ever since: always thoroughly vet the finances before stepping into a leadership role at any nonprofit organization.

Key Life Lesson: Leadership in Crisis Builds Relationships

Chapter 7: Partners and Collaborators to the Rescue

Partners and collaborators aren't just "nice to have" for nonprofit leaders—they're essential to whether a mission can scale, sustain itself, and create lasting change. Nonprofits operate in a landscape defined by limited resources and complex social challenges, so working in isolation is almost always a losing strategy.

Most social issues, such as poverty, educational gaps, homelessness, and climate resilience, are far too large for any single organization to solve. Strong partnerships allow nonprofits to:

- Reach more people
- Deliver more comprehensive services
- Influence systems rather than treat symptoms

A small nonprofit with strong partners can have the impact of a much larger one. Partnerships also bring resources that nonprofits often lack. Few organizations have all the funding, staff capacity, or specialized expertise they need.

Meanwhile, collaborators can contribute:

- Funding
- Volunteers

- Specialized knowledge
- Technology or infrastructure

Collaboration also builds credibility and trust. When a nonprofit partners with respected institutions — universities, hospitals, foundations, government agencies, or peer organizations — it signals legitimacy and strengthens:

- Fundraising efforts
- Community trust
- Policy influence
- Media visibility

Key Life Lesson: Leadership is Relationship; Success is a Shared Reality

Chapter 8: Crisis Management is Coming—Get Ready

If you lead a nonprofit, you *will* face crises at some point in your career. It's almost a rite of passage in the sector. Funding can evaporate overnight, a key partner can collapse, a program can fail publicly, or an internal issue can suddenly become an external one. The question isn't *if* a crisis will happen, but *how prepared you are when it does.*

Crisis Management Story

Early in my career at the Boys and Girls Clubs, I faced a crisis that exposed my inexperience as a leader. I had just stepped into a supervisory role at our camp, and I was determined to prove myself. Instead of building relationships and listening to my team, I came in with a rigid plan and an assumption that authority alone would earn respect. It didn't.

Within weeks, communication broke down. Staff were confused about expectations, frustrated by sudden changes, and increasingly disengaged. Tension grew, morale dropped, and eventually the program itself began to suffer. Parents complained about inconsistencies, staff turnover increased, and the quality of our youth experience slipped.

The breaking point came during a major program week when several staff members didn't show up. I was left scrambling to cover gaps, field parent concerns, and keep the program afloat. It was a moment of truth, and I knew I had created the crisis.

Instead of blaming the team, I went to my Executive Director and admitted that I had mishandled the situation. He listened, then told me something I needed to hear: Leadership isn't about control. It's about clarity, trust, and shared ownership."

That conversation changed everything.

I called a staff meeting and took responsibility for my mistakes. I asked for their honest feedback—and I listened. Together, we rebuilt our communication structure, clarified roles, and created shared goals that everyone could help shape. I also learned to set boundaries and hold people accountable without being authoritarian.

Over the next several weeks, the culture shifted. Staff felt heard, expectations became clearer, and the program stabilized. Parents noticed the improvement, and the team began to take pride in the work again.

That crisis taught me one of the most important lessons of my career: **leadership failure isn't the end—it's an invitation to grow.** It forced me to develop humility, emotional intelligence, and the ability to lead through collaboration rather than command. Those lessons have shaped every leadership role I've held since.

Here are some tips to handle a crisis when it happens.

- Do whatever is necessary to ensure everyone is safe

- Commit to telling the truth about the situation, even if it is uncomfortable
- Have one spokesperson to speak to the public on behalf of the organization, even if it is not the CEO or Executive Director
- Don't overshare and give unnecessary details
- Establish a communication plan that the agency will follow
- Try to get back to a normal routine as quickly as possible
- Communicate with your clients, families, and funders as soon as possible to get ahead of any potential rumors
- Document the entire situation
- Bring in experts as necessary

Key Life Lesson: A culture that acknowledges mistakes as opportunities sustains human-centered commitment and impact

Chapter 9: Self-Care Is a Requirement and not an Elective

Self-care isn't a "nice to have" for a nonprofit leader—it's a strategic necessity. The nonprofit world asks leaders to carry big missions with limited resources, high emotional stakes, and constant pressure to serve others. Without intentional self-care, even the most passionate leader eventually hits a wall.

Here's why it matters so much:

- Nonprofit work is a marathon. Leaders who don't pace themselves burn out, and burnout doesn't just affect them—it ripples through the entire organization. When a leader models healthy boundaries and rest, it normalizes sustainability for the whole team.
- Exhaustion narrows perspective. Rest, reflection, and personal well-being expand it. A leader who is mentally and emotionally grounded makes sharper decisions, navigates crises more effectively, and avoids reactive choices that can derail a mission.
- Nonprofit leaders often absorb the stress, trauma, and urgency of the communities they serve. Self-care builds the emotional buffer needed to stay compassionate without becoming overwhelmed.
- Teams take cues from their leaders. If the leader is constantly overworked, stressed, or unavailable, the culture becomes one of

urgency and depletion. When leaders prioritize well-being, they permit their teams to do the same—and that leads to better retention, morale, and collaboration.

- A depleted leader can't champion a mission with the same clarity, creativity, or energy. Self-care directly supports the organization's ability to innovate, fundraise, build partnerships, and serve its community.

Key Life Lesson: Resilience is built on rest and renewal

Chapter 10: Legacy of a Nonprofit Leader

My legacy will never be defined solely by the programs I launched or the dollars I raised. It lives in the people and communities whose lives were changed along the way. When I look back, I'm struck by what an extraordinary journey it has been.

I often think about my early years at the Boys and Girls Clubs of Detroit. Some of the young people I worked with—now senior citizens—still reach out more than forty years later. They tell me how something I said, or the way I believed in them, shaped the trajectory of their lives. Just three months ago, a former member called to share how she was doing and how the guidance I offered her as a teenager still anchors her today. Moments like these remind me that impact is not always loud or visible; sometimes it's carried quietly in the hearts of the people we serve. I feel like a proud uncle every time I hear from them.

The refrigeration repair program is another legacy I hold close. Through a major contract awarded by CHA, we placed public housing residents in full-time, career-path jobs. I will never forget the day a former gang member approached me at a community event. He said, "You helped take me off the streets. You gave me real skills and the ability to legitimately take care of my family. "You're my hero, and I'll never forget you." His words reminded me that opportunity can be the most powerful form of intervention.

My time at the Chicago Youth Centers was equally transformative. Turning that facility around amid community violence, gang activity, and scarce resources was considered nothing short of legendary. Funders would walk in expecting chaos and instead find a spotless building, no graffiti, and vibrant programming. They would ask, almost in disbelief, "How are you operating so effectively with all these barriers?" My answer was always the same: our team was composed of community members deeply committed to the mission. They weren't chasing paychecks—they were chasing change.

Because the YMCA and Chicago Youth Center were less than a mile apart, residents saw the combined impact of my work in both places. Many spoke of my leadership as if I were a local celebrity. In their eyes, I was a big deal, and they showed me a level of respect that I never took for granted.

And then came my final chapter in the Englewood community. Leading the Quality-of-Life Plan process brought together thousands of residents to shape the future of their neighborhood. That collective effort led to real, measurable change: a million-dollar grant to launch a major public safety initiative; the Englewood Police Youth Baseball League, which transformed an unused park and earned national recognition for bridging youth and police; and the arrival of a Whole Foods Market, which sparked a Business Plan Competition where the CEO personally invested in local entrepreneurs. These were not just programs; they were catalysts for hope, dignity, and opportunity.

Honestly, I could talk for hours about the many moments, partnerships, and victories that shaped my journey. But I'll stop here. My legacy lives in the people, the places, and the possibilities we created together—and that is more than enough.

Key Life Lesson: Legacy results from enduring relationships borne of meaningful engagement.

Conclusion:

Looking back over the decades, I realize that my true legacy isn't found in buildings, budgets, or titles. It lives in the people whose lives were touched, the communities that grew stronger, and the opportunities that took root because someone believed that change was possible. My journey has been shaped by countless faces, stories, and moments—each one a reminder that leadership is ultimately an act of service.

From Detroit to Chicago, from youth centers to citywide initiatives, I witnessed what can happen when communities are empowered, when people are given a chance, and when leaders choose compassion over convenience. I saw young people grow into adults who still carried the lessons we shared. I saw former gang members become providers for their families. I saw neighborhoods come together to imagine a better future—and then build it.

If there is one thread that ties my work together, it is this: **impact multiplies when you invest in people**. Programs may evolve, buildings may change hands, and organizations may shift direction, but the lives touched along the way continue to ripple outward.

I am grateful for every challenge, every partnership, and every victory—big or small. My story is not just about what I accomplished, but about what we accomplished together. And if my journey proves anything, it's that one committed leader, working alongside a determined community, can spark transformation that lasts long after the work is done.

That is the legacy I leave behind, and it has been the honor of a lifetime.

Author's Bio

Perry L. Gunn is a nonprofit executive leader born and raised on the South Side of Chicago, where his deep commitment to youth development and community empowerment first took shape. With more than three decades of experience, he has become a respected voice in neighborhood revitalization, organizational leadership, and community engagement across the Midwest.

He currently serves as CEO of the Nonprofit Membership Club, consulting with and coaching organizations in Chicago, Indianapolis, and throughout the region. Before this role, he led Teamwork Englewood as Executive Director, retiring in 2019 after guiding the Englewood Quality of Life Planning process—an ambitious, community-driven blueprint focused on education and youth, economic development, housing, health and wellness, and public safety.

A lifelong youth practitioner, Gunn began his career with the Boys and Girls Clubs, creating opportunities that supported the social and emotional growth of thousands of young people. His leadership continued at the YMCA of Metropolitan Chicago, where he served as Youth Program Director, Executive Director, and Vice President of Operations. He became known for bringing high-quality programming to underserved neighborhoods and for launching innovative initiatives, including a community-wide tutoring program to address literacy gaps and a refrigeration repair program that created jobs while supporting residents managing diabetes.

Gunn also held senior leadership roles with Chicago Youth Centers as Executive Director, Area Director, and Regional Executive Director. Across these positions, he built a reputation for mobilizing volunteers, cultivating philanthropic partnerships, and strengthening community-based institutions.

He holds a Master of Arts in Inner City Studies from Northeastern Illinois University and a Bachelor of Science from George Williams College. He serves on the Board of Imagine Englewood If and on the Leadership Council of Growing Home, an urban agriculture organization. He is also a Leadership Greater Chicago Fellow.

His work has been recognized with numerous honors, including the University of Chicago's Nonprofit Impact Award, the Leader of Excellence Award, the Legacy Award, and the Englewood Heroes Award.

Made in the USA
Monee, IL
04 November 2026

67381927R00024